THE MISSION

A TRUE STORY TOLD THROUGH THE EYES OF THE ANIMALS

SECOND EDITION

By DOREEN INGRAM

ILLUSTRATIONS BY JOSH GREEN

Other Books by Doreen Ingram

My Sanctuary
Keepers of the Wild
Squirrelly Sally

Ingram Swanson & Company, LLC.
2831 St. Rose Parkway, Suite 450
Henderson, NV 89052

www.myplacecalledhome.com

ISBN: 978-0-9913571-5-4

DEDICATION

Chimpanzees in the wild are disappearing fast. This book is dedicated to all the people and sanctuaries involved in stopping the rapid loss and abuse of our precious wildlife, and to the chimps that have survived unbelievable abuse and neglect.

Helping to educate our next generation and adults about the animals' plight, while trying to instill empathy, is an important part of my books.

"Captures the desperate need of orphaned chimpanzees and how they find love and a new life at Chimp Eden. The perfect gift for every child."

—Jane Goodall, PhD, DBE
Founder, the Jane Goodall Institute and UN Messenger of Peace

CONTENTS

ACKNOWLEDGMENTS

A special thank you to sanctuary manager and primate expert, Phillip Cronje, for all his updates and assistance as I wrote this second book.

David Devo Oosthuizen was the photographer whose beautiful live shots were used in this book. Thank you for all you do for animals and the chimps. His work was donated for use in this book.

Marc Cronje was especially wonderful by sending me video and pictures he took so Josh could create the artwork.

My tribute is also to all the veterinarians around the world who give so much of their time and love to animals. This is why a veterinarian was used for the front cover.

Thank you to all the staff at the Jane Goodall Institute of South Africa and Chimp Eden.

Many thanks go to the team at Aqua Vision Wildlife filmmakers for their help in the mission to save the chimps while filming a documentary, and for allowing me to use some of their pictures for artwork. Thank you, Jaco.

Eugene Cussons' love for chimps and desire to help them is appreciated, and I wanted to give him and his family a big thank you also. Chimp Eden is a beautiful place to visit and for the chimps to live.

Josh Green's hard work shows in the pictures he drew, and they are beautiful.

Kimberly Gordon helped in some pre-editing and is an amazing author of many great stories.

Again, I am so thankful to Dr. Jane Goodall for her work with and dedication to chimpanzees.

Chapter 1

RISE AND SHINE!

"Joao! Wake up! You're dreaming again, Joao!"

I could hear his voice, but my eyelids weren't quite ready to focus on the brightness of the day yet. He put his foot on my arm, and that did it.

"Okay, Cozy! I'm up."

Yeah, it was one of those bad dreams. I still have them every once in awhile. Running through the forest, away from the bad things I have experienced in my long life.

But today I don't need to run away from anything. I'm happy.

So as my eyes begin to open and I notice my family beginning to move about, stretch, and awaken…we wait.

My family and I are waiting to hear the vehicle come down the road. Every morning they come—the people who take care of us here at our sanctuary home.

Until they come, we lounge sleepily in our beds of straw. Except for the birds singing out their morning songs, things are quiet.

Ah, there they are! Our keepers are coming. We can all hear the engine of the Land Rover and the sound of the tires on the road. Things aren't quiet anymore. Our whole family is hooting and hollering with excitement. What a racket! Cozy kicks the steel door of our night room where we sleep, then Zac kicks it even harder just to make a point.

Breakfast is here. Our keepers have arrived!

Last night, I shared some of my dinner with Sampa who, by the way, is still a great mum figure to Tony and the rest of the family, so I'm really hungry this morning. It's a good thing we are fed five times a day here. Chimps are always hungry.

I can hear the humans talking now. Phillip is here! He is the alpha male of the sanctuary. I believe humans call him the sanctuary manager. We are chimpanzees, from the great ape family. That includes chimps, bonobos, gorillas, and orangutans. Sadly, there aren't many of us left. We will become extinct in the wild if something isn't done soon, is what I've heard tell. I know it to be a fact, because my whole family was killed when I was a baby.

Doors are opening now, and we can go outside. Phillip's there to greet us as we exit the night rooms. It is good to see our human family this morning. What a beautiful day it is; it's sunny and warm here in South Africa. My stomach is rumbling now, so I'll go in search of the food our keepers have put out for us. If I hurry, I might get a papaya or maybe even an eggplant. Yum!

Zac gets first pick, though. He's our leader now. I am still a high-ranking member, but age has slowed me down, and it's time to rest more. They still call me Granddad but, of course, my real name is Joao.

Now Zac has the job of disciplining the family in our enclosure. I help out when I can, playing with the little ones and keeping them in line, but I have done my job, so I leave the real work for Zac. Like most granddads, I prefer a good nap.

As I pick up my fruit and vegetables, I can keep an eye on our forest sanctuary. There are many trees but some open grassy spaces, too. In the distance, I can see a zebra family. They are also eating, with their heads dropped to the ground as they nibble on fresh spring grass. There are four, including a young foal and its mother.

I like their colors, black and white, which are impressive against the green bushes and tan-colored hills.

Swinging in the trees, above the zebras, is a troop of vervet monkeys. They are different from me; they have tails.

You see, monkeys have tails; apes do not. They seem very excited, swinging through the high branches with such grace!

One just broke a branch off a very tall tree, and down it came, crashing to the ground. Oh, well…so much for the grace part.

I can see a mother vervet monkey with her baby hanging onto her back for dear life. She has spotted their breakfast, and she is swinging down toward the food, using her arms, legs, and tail to grab the branches. They really move quite fast!

The troop has spotted some bread that was left on the grounds, and that is a treat, so I guess that's what all the excitement's about. Usually, the vervet monkeys eat what we do, which includes flowers, fruits, vegetables, plant bulbs, roots, seeds,

4

and the bark from some trees. We all love insects, grubs, and bird eggs as well as a few other things.

The vervet monkeys are much smaller than I am. Their faces are small and black, with a white band on their forehead, and their body hair can be gray or greenish- olive in color. The newborn babies are so cute. They have tiny pink faces and black fur. They stay close to their mothers because the danger of being taken and killed by a hawk, eagle, or another predator is always present. That's called *nature*.

Ah! Something has just flown past me, bringing my thoughts back to the morning. It was a rock! Who did it? Usually, it's Cozy, but no…I see it was Zac. He has too much energy today and might be in a bad mood.

"Watch out!" I just called out to some of the babies standing too close to Zac's target. Zac is still at it, throwing another huge rock. That one almost hits the Land Rover as

5

our keepers are driving to another enclosure. It is easy for Zac to toss boulders in the air, because chimps are at least six times stronger than humans, which I must admit, I'm proud to say.

I'll give Zac a hug, and it will surely calm him down for now. We do that, and it shows our close bond with each other; sometimes it's to give reassurance that everything is okay. Maybe that's all he needs this morning, reassurance.

Cozy, like I mentioned earlier, enjoys throwing rocks, too. Visitors come to the Jane Goodall Sanctuary to get an idea about our lives before and after our rescues.

Cozy likes humans, well…mostly. Sometimes he gets upset, though, and doesn't really know what to do or how to behave like a normal chimpanzee. To get their attention, he will give them a big mouth grin, showing off all of his beautiful teeth. He'll also throw a stone or two and puff up his hair to make himself look bigger than he really is. Then he'll clap his hands really hard and loud. It gets their attention!

Honestly, this is bad behavior, but I love Cozy anyway. He is one of a kind, and I know he had many years of abuse and neglect before he came here. We just ignore the bad behavior most of the time, because Cozy loves the little chimps, takes very good care of them, and is really quite helpful. Tony is especially good pals with Cozy. You will see them together most of the time.

My favorite time of the day here is our twelve o'clock tour of visitors because, during that time, we get macadamia nuts and peanuts. It's definitely my favorite time of day!

§ § § § § §

Snack time is over, my group is happily playing, climbing trees, and just hanging out. I think I'll rest under the shade of this eucalyptus tree that stands tall near the corner of my enclosure. It is out of the way of the little ones playing, and I am ready for some quite time. From here, I can see and hear my group and another group in the next enclosure.

I close my eyes, but it isn't long before the sound of someone approaching disturbs my relaxation.

It happens to be Jessica, she is the alpha female and oldest chimp in the enclosure next to mine. It looks as though she is eager to tell me something.

"Joao," she says, somewhat breathless. "Joao, he's coming!"

"Who?" I ask. "Who is coming, Jessica?"

"Charles! He's here to join my family. Charles has gone through his quarantine time and will meet everyone soon."

With that, she disappears from sight as fast as she had appeared just a few moments ago.

When Jessica arrived at our sanctuary home, she was a pitiful sight. There were cigarette burns all over her chest and arms—signs of abuse by her owners. How horrible! She was emaciated, too. That means she was very thin and weak. *Starved* might be another way of putting it. She sure has come a long way since then.

Now, she is a wonderful mum to all the orphans in her enclosure and a good alpha, or female, leader to the older ones in the group. Besides Jessica, there are ten more members in her enclosure, and they are named Mowgli, Tamu, Lilly, Bazia, Charlene, Azzie, Mary, Marco, Suzie, and Martha.

Tamu is one of the youngest ones, but he thinks he is a big chimp. He struts around like he is the big male of the group, walking on his knuckles with wide-spread arms. Since he still has his little white tuft of hair on his backside, he is still considered a baby, but don't tell him that.

All the babies have that tuft until they are four to six years old. It is there to let everyone know that they are still learning and are to be given special care and encouragement.

While strolling down the fence line to the next corner, I hear that familiar voice again. Lilly and Charlene, two of the babies in Jessica's enclosure, are playing with a stick. Jessica is talking with them, so I think I'll sit close enough to chat more about her mystery chimp, Charles.

"Jessica, will you tell me more about Charles? Obviously, you knew him before you came here. I'm a good listener," I tell her. "I'm all ears to hear why you're so excited. Share with me your experience; that is, if you're up to it?" I say, interested to hear more.

Jessica takes a deep, slow breath and then lets out a soft sigh. "Well, Joao, I lived for a very long time, locked away in a cage in a dark and lonely room where I could

barely make out shadows. I was part of a circus as a baby chimp. When I got too big and strong, the owners got scared of me. I couldn't help it! When people teased me or treated me badly, I would scream and throw tantrums. The masters didn't like that, so they locked me away. When they did come in to feed me, they would be mean and hit me with a cold metal rod they carried with them for their protection. It hurt. They hit me until I would get into the corner of the cage.

"At times, they would burn me with their cigarettes and laugh at me when I screamed. And as you know, I still have the scars to this day.

"One time, the master came in. He was angry. One of my hands was grasping at a bar on my cage. He took a sharp object and slammed it on my hand. I lost three fingers that day," she says to me sadly.

"I don't know how long I lay on the floor, but when I woke up, I was very weak. I don't believe I have ever recovered from that scary time. Anyway, Charles was in the same dark room as I was. I couldn't see him, but I knew he was there. We knew each other when we were young and entertained the people at the circus. Even though we were in separate cages, we could still hear each other, and that was a comfort to me. I thought I would never see him again. Today, I heard his familiar voice. I never forget a voice, Joao. It was Charles, and I know he will be introduced to my family group tomorrow, because I heard the keepers talking about it. What a surprise it will be for Charles to see me again. Oh…I will not sleep tonight; I'm so excited!"

Well…it was good to know the whole story, so with that, I bid Jessica a good day, and now I will go and lie in the soft grass.

She has given me much to think about. Something inside me is stirring. A change is coming. I can feel it. I search the blue sky above, wondering what this change might be. Something is coming…soon. But for now, I have to WAIT.

Chapter 2

THE GIFT

I am still awake tonight, but it isn't that I'm not tired—I am. I drift in and out of consciousness as the feeling of change continues to taunt me. The only noise in this dark night is the occasional screeching of the great owl outside in the woods. He is letting all creatures, great and small, know that this is his time to lay claim over his territory. I just listen. Things are quiet this minute, but I am fully awake now. My eyes will not close. My heart is pounding slightly faster than usual. I don't know why. I roll over to my other side.

My turning disturbs Cozy. He raises his head, so I just grunt, and he lowers it back down, realizing everything is okay. Nothing is wrong, so why do I feel anxious? Then it comes to me—the thing that I must do, or that must be done. I don't know how it shall be done, but I have faith that it will. FAITH has gotten me this far in life. It was faith that told me I would see brighter days, and I have. Every day, I find something good in life. That's it; now I understand this change, and it will be good. Now, maybe I can sleep.

§ § § § §

As I awaken, I see that the day is much like any other day. It is indeed glorious, with the sun shining and the sky so clear you can see all the hills and mountains in the distance.

The wind is blowing softly, and it is very warm. This is my favorite kind of day, and I believe it will be a special one for sure.

So, after the ten o'clock tour and our second meal of the day, I go over to my corner near the woods to lie down and take in some sunshine for awhile. Sometimes I still sit on my favorite tree stump, or the logs, but I'm enjoying the soft, warm, spring grasses right now.

I have heard a lot of noise coming from Jessica's camp, and I am pretty sure I know what is going on there. I even got to see Eugene, and that's always a treat. Phillip and the keepers are introducing Charles, the newest member of that group, today. I am happy that another chimp has made it out of a life of misery and into this wonderful sanctuary.

After awhile, Jessica comes over to share the news with me. "Joao," she says. "It's wonderful! He is the same Charles I have known for so long. He's quiet and depressed right now, I'm afraid, but I know I can help him, and he WILL get better!"

While I listen to Jessica talk, I turn from her and look up. I notice how clear and blue the sky is—extremely blue and clear. I spot two black crows sitting on a fence near us. They are black as the night, but when their feathers shine in the sunlight, they have an almost purple hue. The colors all around seem unnatural, almost unreal—deep blues, purples, reds, and greens. I am beginning to think I have eaten something I shouldn't have! My heart is beating just slightly faster again, and it reminds me of the way I felt last night.

It's time.

I know it is. "But how?" I ask myself. My mind is racing. What is going on inside of me? I feel strange.

Jessica is looking at me with a questioning expression. No words, just looking. Does she know what I am thinking? Does she think I have become ill? She looks a little pale.

Do I look *pale?*

Just now, as I look back up to the sky, I see a sparrow hawk flying over both of us, letting out a shrill cry, *cawww cawww.*

It is a standard hawk call, as those things go. But when I look into Jessica's now very wide eyes, I know that isn't just an ordinary hawk or cry. It is special.

"Jessica," I say, "I need to tell you something. It's important."

"I, uh, I will have your voice, Joao, won't I?" she asks a bit nervously. "The *voice* to carry on the stories and teaching to all who will listen. But why? Why can't you continue what you have been given?" she asks.

"I don't know why, Jessica," I say. "But it is yours now, and you must share our stories so others can learn about our plight. The hawk did his job; now you must do yours. Your heart is still full of love and hope, and you have more to give. It's time for me to rest and watch now. I pass this gift on to you. I am fulfilled and truly at peace."

Jessica's eyes are watching me as I move away from my corner of the woods. I go slowly to an area where some of the younger chimps are playing. I lay my head down on the green grass and peacefully rest, now that the "voice" is safe with Jessica.

He deserves the peace, I think to myself. Yes…I have the voice now. This is a gift, and I am so grateful! I can think to myself and share my thoughts with those who will listen.

I must get back to Charles now and tell him what has happened to me. I hope he will understand. If not, he will in time. I will make sure of that!

§ § § § §

Much later in the day, as I make my way back to our night rooms, I spot Martha sitting high up in a tree, looking down at me. She does not communicate much yet and will not groom with most of the others, except for Lilly. Lilly is able to get close to her and likes to follow Martha around. I think Martha likes that, even though she doesn't show a lot of emotion. She is still getting used to being around other chimpanzees.

Martha came from a country in Africa called Ghana. As with many of the chimps that end up in sanctuaries or zoos, Martha was a pet when she was a baby. She was given to a zoo once she got too big to handle, and she didn't get along well with the other chimps, since she wasn't used to being around them. Instead of working to get her to be part of the chimp group, the people gave up and put her in a cage by herself. That is where she lived for many years.

Martha, I think, will learn to enjoy her newfound family more and more as time goes by. But for now, I give her space and allow her to keep to herself as she wishes.

As for the babies, they really want someone to be their mum. They especially enjoy being close to us older girls, but I watch over all of them carefully.

Even yesterday, I watched Tamu explore the new water hole that was put into our enclosure. Our keepers call it a *pool,* and it gets filled with water each day. The babies have found this very entertaining, especially Tamu. He decided he was the only one who would be allowed in it for awhile. He twirled and twirled around in that pool and, at one point, he made his own bubbles. You could say he had air in his tummy that had to come out! Either way, he had lots of fun, and we had fun watching him. I even heard laughter coming from the keepers, too! Eventually, the other babies got a chance to put their arm or leg in the water, and they enjoyed throwing sticks and dirt in the pool.

Today, it is hot, and sometimes water does feel good, though many older chimps do not like getting wet. There are always exceptions, though. Suzie seems to like the water and will even get into the spray as the keepers are cleaning out the night rooms. Like I said, there are always exceptions to the rule.

Suzie was kept on a chain near the beach in Angola. People teased her badly. But even with all that behind her, she enjoys humans and chimps alike.

She has really become a wonderful big sister to the babies here, and she watches and learns from me. I have even seen her carry Charlene around, acting as if she was a mum. I know that if she were in the wild today, she would be a great mum.

Well, it's time to go inside now. There are dark clouds moving in, and the wind is beginning to blow quite strongly. Changing weather is just a part of life here in South Africa. It's sunny for awhile, and a rainstorm soon after is not unusual during some of the seasons.

So…into the night rooms we go! I have had quite an interesting day today. I wonder, what will tomorrow bring?

I watch as Charles slowly comes in. He and I will share a room by ourselves tonight, since we've been friends for so long. That is a good thing, because it will give me time to do some much-needed grooming with him and maybe get him to relax a little and talk to me. I just hope he understands that he is here from now on and forever. He will never have to go back to any bad place again. He has a new home at this sanctuary, as we all do, and we will never have to suffer at the

hands of bad humans again. We have been promised that, and I trust our human caretakers.

TRUST...like Joao would say, that is a good word! That in itself is truly a gift.

Chapter 3

THE STORM

Even though there are heavy covers over the windows of our night rooms, I can still see the flashes of light outside. The lightning is very bright! The loud, booming sounds of thunder follow each crackling flash. The babies are scared in their room next to mine, but I encourage them to stay calm. Eventually, they will fall asleep, piled high on top of one another for protection. It is such a cute sight but, naturally, Mum and baby would be a much better combination. Here we do what we're able to do.

Morning has arrived, and all is well. When the keepers open the night room

doors, all of us go out except for Charles. I call out to him, but he is just sitting in the room that we shared last night. I suppose he is bewildered by this new place. Thinking that it might help, I return to the room and begin grooming him. It is relaxing for me to pick through the hairs on his neck and arms, checking for insects and dirt left from the day before. All I have found, though, is some straw from where he slept last night. The grooming must feel good to him though, because he has gotten up and followed me outside. The sky has cleared up, but there are limbs and leaves everywhere from the storm.

I think I'll take a little stroll now that I'm done with my breakfast. I climb to the top of a tree that has been broken in the storm. It is leaning over the fence, so I'll just go on over and hop down on the other side. I stop for a moment and realize that I am outside of my enclosure. Hey…you only live once, right?

I wonder what is over the hill? I know I might not get another chance to find out, so I think I'll go exploring.

Curious to see more, I walk down the dirt road, up and over a small hill. It surprises me to gaze upon land with no fences or buildings as far as the eye can see! I feel out of place, I am slowly losing my courage to continue my investigation, but I keep moving. I see a herd of impala walking slowly through some small bushes and grasses. They are

such pretty animals with big, brown eyes and horns on their head. I can't wait to share this adventure with my chimpanzee family.

As I think about this, something startles the impala, and they begin to run. It doesn't take me long to realize what has scared them. I am getting scared, too! A troop of baboons is coming down over the hill right toward me! There is nowhere to run and no trees to climb. A tree won't help me anyway; baboons are good climbers, too. There are seven of them and only one of me. I am beginning to feel a little panicked, so I'm just going to turn around and walk slowly back to where I have just come from. Uh, oh! Now one of the baboons has run around and is right in front of me. I know I am in real

trouble now! I don't know what to do. The big male is showing his teeth; that is not a good sign. I can feel my body begin to shake, and I see that they are coming closer and closer to me.

Normally, baboons and chimps are not enemies. However, I think this group is still a little upset over an incident that happened recently. One of their family members got into our chimpanzee enclosure, and we ran him out. We were pretty mean about it, and he was upset at the time. But here, the situation is reversed. I am in their territory and too old to outrun them. They are all in better shape than I am, because they are wild and have never been abused like I was. My legs are going weak, and I am very nervous knowing that I am running out of time.

I hear a noise behind me. "Jessica, are you all right?" Charles calls out.

I am so relieved. "Charles, I am in a bit of a situation right now!" my shaky voice answers.

The baboon blocking my way is showing his big, scary teeth. They are sharp canines, big and dangerous. Charles stands on two legs and puffs up his fur, so he actually looks quite big. He and I both let out an alarm call. In the distance, our chimp family hears us and responds loudly to our calls. The baboons finally feel threatened and outnumbered, so they decide to be smart and leave us alone. In fact, they run away.

Whew! That was a close call. "Let's go home," I tell Charles. The hair on his back is back to normal and he gives me a satisfied glance. I am a lucky chimp, thankful for a good friend today.

"After you, madam," he replies kindly.

§ § § § §

As you might imagine, now that we have gotten back, we are on the wrong side of the fence! As we walk closer to the buildings, we can hear some of the keepers calling out our names. Themba spots us and cautiously approaches me. I accept his hand and walk on two legs toward the night rooms. Charles follows. On our way, I am pleased to see a new face. It is the young chimp that I have been hearing about lately, but have not seen. She is a pretty little female, young, but not a baby.

Marc, the son of Phillip, is standing near the pathway. He has just finished a tour and is coming to check on this new chimp and bring her a meal. "This is Claudine," he says, looking my way. Themba continues to walk us through the doors until we are safely back in our enclosure.

I am happy to learn that she will soon be joining Joao's family group. What a lucky chimp! I do not know her story, but I'm sure it is not a happy one. I know that Eugene and the team rescued her. Thankfully, she has made her way here with their help. That is a very good thing.

It has been quite a day. I have learned to stay on my side of the big fence from now on. What would the babies do if something had happened to me? Charles would have been upset, too, if he had not been able to find me. Joao would have been disappointed as well, and I wouldn't want that to ever happen! I know I'll sleep well tonight, now that I'm safe again.

§ § § § § §

Charles and I have spent a lot of time together over the past few days, grooming and watching the babies. I can just tell that he is going to make a great dad and alpha of this family group. Just when I think things are returning to normal, the sparrow hawk makes another appearance. This time, he perches on the lower limb of the tree I am sitting under.

He has never spoken to me before, but his call turns into words that I can understand. "My name is Moomba," he says. "I have news for you, Jessica." I watch as he flies closer and lands on the rock beside me. "I will be leaving for a time," he

says. "A mission, if you will. I will be bringing you news of a new one that will be calling this his home."

"A new one?" I ask. "Do you mean we will have a new chimp brought here, to live?"

"Yes, Jessica. He is a very lonely chimp who has been living in an old abandoned zoo. He doesn't have long, because he might be killed if no one can take him. He is too big and strong to be let out of his cage, and people fear him now. There may be other chimps in the country that might be able to be rescued, but I'm not sure right now."

"Oh, the poor boy! You must go and do what you can. Please!"

"I will, but I must use the voice you have been given. I promise it will be returned to you, Jessica."

"Yes, Moomba. Do what you have to do. Bring this new one here safely and tell all who will listen about your journey. I will wait for the news, but return swiftly and safely."

"That I shall do, Jessica. I will return, and there will be a celebration!"

§ § § § §

These last several days have been very busy here at our sanctuary home. I see many new faces. Moomba says that these humans will be part of the big mission. One of the humans, in particular, can speak in a different language. I believe they call it *Afrikaans,* and it is the secondary language spoken here in South Africa. I actually do not understand it, because I am not from this country originally. Chimpanzees are not naturally from South Africa; they have been brought here. This sanctuary was prepared for orphans, abused, and neglected chimps, and it is the only one in this country. Thank goodness for a human lady named Dr. Jane Goodall, who has worked for over fifty years with chimpanzees. Without her work and dedication to chimps everywhere, I don't know where we would be.

Anyway, one of these new faces is a man with strawberry-blond-colored hair. He is carrying some tools around his neck, pointing them at us from time to time. I am laughing at some of his poses as he does his work. I don't believe he realizes how entertaining he is, but we certainly aren't scared of him or his assistants. They speak to us tenderly and have good smiles on their faces. Phillip calls these men the "film crew," whatever that means. The other man with the tools on his neck calls out for his "Nikon." I also hear the words *photography* and *Sony 750 HD.* I guess these tools are important for the mission that Moomba told me about. Whatever it is, I will have to be patient and find out later.

In the meantime, I will take care of this family and look after Charles. He is getting strong and continues to work toward being the leader of this group. In fact, Charles is watching Tamu right now. It's a good thing Tamu still has his little white tuft on his bum, because if he didn't, he might just get a bad scolding from Charles right now! Tamu just ran through the entrance of the night rooms, holding a big stick in one hand, hitting the walls along the way, and making as much noise as he can so everyone will be aware that he is here. I guess it's time for bed. Good night!

Chapter 4

THE MISSION: SAVE THE CHIMPS

Morning is here. My family and I are enjoying a breakfast of ripe bananas, oranges, and peaches. The sky is blue and clear with a few fluffy clouds moving slowly overhead.

I hear the call I have been anticipating. I am excitedly looking around for Moomba. I spot him circling high above me. With his loud call, I instinctively know that it is time to pass the "voice" to this brave hawk. Now Moomba can share with the world the things I will not be able to see.

So Moomba's journey begins. Let's hear what he has to say…

§ § § § §

This is all new to me, and I am pleased that Jessica is selfless and gracious enough to trust me with this gift! I must leave now to get a good start. I must not fall too far behind the airplane that will take the team to the country where there is so much chaos and danger at every turn! We are going to the Central African Republic, or CAR for short. It is very unstable, with war and tragedy happening every day for humans and animals alike. It is a country with beautiful scenery and many species of plants and animals, but it is still a dangerous one. I will go and follow these brave humans into this land, share their adventures and stories, and, hopefully, bring a few chimpanzees home that are in need of help.

Feeling a little anxious and excited at the same time, I fly away from my home to new territory. I spot many small shacks with tin roofs, large farms with fruit trees, papaya plants, rows of pineapple plants, vegetable gardens, and lots of vehicles and roads.

I fly over desertlike areas that look like they have been burned out, but now have new green plant life sprouting up everywhere. Flying along a river, I glide lower to take a glance at a hippopotamus family basking in the sun. Momma hippo is keeping a close eye on her baby, because there is a crocodile nearby. The baby would be in danger without its mum's protection, but the crocodile would not attempt to fight with a protective mother hippo! Well, I'd better get on with it. Enough sightseeing. I have quite a long trip, and there are clouds rolling in, so I'm turning on the power and my instincts will guide me to the place I need to go.

§ § § § §

Finally, I have arrived. My trip has been long and exhausting, but I have managed to get to the place where Phillip, Jaco, Hanru, Skye, and Dr. Stephen van der Spuy are located. Dr. Stephen is a veterinarian—a doctor who takes care of animals. He and Phillip are here to make sure the chimps are cared for properly. I have been listening intently to their conversations, and Dr. Stephen will have to use a needle and syringe to get some blood samples from the chimps to make sure they do not have simian AIDS or other diseases. If they do, they will not be able to come to our home.

The team is staying near the capital city of Bangui, and it is far, far away from my home in Nelspruit. The weather here is much warmer and more humid than I am used to. The team looks sweaty and uncomfortable, too, but they are here for a mission, and it seems they are willing to endure much to save these chimps.

First thing in the morning, we will start our search at an abandoned zoo in Bangui. They believe there is a six-year-old chimp there named Claude. The team also has to get the permits from the government so Claude can leave the country.

It's my time to rest, so I will sit on a wire I have found that runs close to the house where the team will sleep. I will catch some food early in the morning to give me the energy I will need to follow the vehicles to their destinations.

§ § § § §

Morning has come, and the sun peeks through the clouds. I have awakened early, caught some breakfast, and now watch as the team moves to the vehicles parked near the house where they slept. There is a new vehicle waiting for them, with more people who look different from our team. They wear uniforms. I am apprehensive, but I take flight and stay in close range of the team as they pull out into the rocky and unkempt roads of this city. I fly above at a fair pace as the vehicles travel quite a ways to their destination—Bangui Zoo grounds.

Hmm…not much here at the zoo but some pieces and parts of old and dilapidated cages with vines, grasses, and trees growing over and through most of the area. We come to a cage that is about the size of one of the vehicles the team was driving, but just a bit taller. Wow! That is what poor Claude lives in? It's not a nice floor either; it's hard and looks uncomfortable, and there is nothing to play with or climb on. I don't think I could take it for a day, much less years. My heart just aches to think how Claude has lived for most of his life. He was surely a product of the bushmeat trade.

34

One by one, the team members visit with Claude. Each one brings him a piece of fruit, smiles, and speaks tenderly to him. They sit with him for a short time, and I can see by Claude's attentiveness and expression that he is interested in his new friends and enjoys their company. When we start to leave, Claude's hands grip the bars on his cage tightly. I can see the muscles in his arms slightly bulge with tension, a sure sign of stress. I believe that he is thinking that these visitors are leaving him alone again. It is pretty sad to leave him here, even though I know we will be back. I hear the team say we are taking him home, but Claude does not know this yet.

It is beginning to sprinkle a bit, so it is time to go. Besides, nighttime is not a safe time to be out in this part of the country. There is unrest here, like I said before, and there are many people with guns who are not afraid to jump a car and take it from you. This is a place where many people have nothing—no work, little food, and little hope. Maybe that will change one day. If that changes, maybe the way animals are treated here will change, too. That is a good goal. Maybe this is a start?

Anyway, I make my way back to the house and perch right outside the door. I stay as close to the house as possible, because I do not feel safe here at all. I will try to sleep, because I hear that we have a long trip into town tomorrow to locate two little babies that are being used as a tourist attraction at a hotel. I will catch me some winks and hopefully wake with enough energy for a long day.

Chapter 5

CRISIS IN BANGUI

Loud engines of vehicles leaving the residence drown out the sweet sounds of the birds this morning. The roads are in disrepair and, at times, make the trip treacherous. The team is on their way to the city of Bangui.

We are here. It is very busy, congested, and noisy with many small cars and trucks, but many people are traveling on foot, too. Outside of the government buildings, I rest and wait with some of the group. The remainder of the team is inside, talking with government people about permits for

bringing the chimps home. Our stress level is increasing, and each minute feels like an hour.

I'm not sure how long we have waited, but each hour that goes by makes everyone more anxious as we anticipate the news. We all want to know if the papers are in place that would award the chimps to the sanctuary. The hand of the clock turns ever so slowly.

Finally, I spot some of the men coming our way from the tall, cement building. Everyone is beginning to get into the vehicles once again. It is a good sound when I hear the engines start up, but I can see on the faces of the team members that something is not quite right. I see no smiles. In fact, heads are lowered, and it looks like the meeting has not gone well. Flying closer, I catch a bit of the conversation. It seems that there are two baby chimps that may not be able to make it home because of the lack of permits.

"Well…" I hear one of the team members ask, "What are we going to do now?"

Then I hear Phillip answer that they will try to talk to the lady who owns the baby chimps. She owns hotels and uses the baby chimps as an attraction to make money. If they can convince her that the chimps are in danger of getting sick or hurt, and will soon be too big and strong to be with people, maybe she will agree to release the babies to the care of the Jane Goodall Institute.

Jaco says, "It's worth a try!"

I follow the vehicles, once again for many hours. We just arrived at a place that looks like a house. I see what I believe is one of the baby chimps. Yes, it is a chimp. Some of the team members have left their vehicles and gone to the door.

A man has come out, and they have all gone to see the chimps that are chained on the side of this yard. It is a terrible mess, and the chimps are on a very short chain. Their names are Tubo and Babush. Oh…all the trash around them is awful, and they sit in the dirt on the ground! They are very young and small and do not look happy at all. The chimps have been stolen from their mothers and families, only to be chained up and used to make money for the hotel owners. They are passed from person to person to get their picture taken and get a hug from perfect strangers.

Hmm…I didn't think this would affect me like this. Their faces, they're so pitiful. I wonder if humans really think that hugging one of these babies is worth all their suffering.

From what I overheard earlier, the team had already spoken to the lady who owns Tubo and Babush this morning. She refuses to give them up. Now as I look on while these babies are chained firmly to an old, rusted car, chewing on some Styrofoam, well, it has broken everyone's heart. I see tears in the eyes of these big, brave men. As they each say goodbye and leave little Tubo and Babush, I can tell they are leaving with heavy hearts. I hear someone say to the others, "We will come back!"

Now we've returned to Claude at the old abandoned zoo. He looks a bit confused and excited. I don't think he was expecting us to return, and I know the team is pleased that he is still here and still looking well.

They are cautious with Claude because he is a wild animal, and he is very strong. But he is calm and has such a friendly personality. It will help him a lot when he meets his new family.

Since nothing too exciting is going on right now, I think I'll relax and have a look around the area. Lifting my wings, I take off into the sky. A short distance away, I hear something like a waterfall. I'll go there. There are interesting bright green plants that surround the rocky waterfall, along with some colorful flowers that add to the beauty of it.

It's amazing how a country can be so beautiful in one place, then, just a few miles away, can be war-torn and in terrible condition. Places like this could disappear forever without good people to take care of it. There is still a rain forest near this area. A few wild chimpanzee families live there. Poaching is a problem. Too many people still want to buy endangered wildlife, even though they know it's wrong. I suppose Tubo and Babush were taken not too far from this area.

I know all this, because I have been listening to the stories that Jaco, Skye, and Hanru have been telling about a time they went into the rain forest for a couple of days. They wanted to get some movie footage and hopefully see some wild chimpanzees. Jaco said that they had come in contact with some hunters in the rain forest who had been stalking the chimps. Quietly and slowly, the hunters made their way through the thick, damp, insect-infested jungle. They hacked through the vines with their knives while listening for the sounds of chimps and looking for any nests that had been built the night before. They also searched for any signs that chimps

had been eating the nearby vegetation or fruits. While the hunters would make camp, all the chimps would be watching and keeping an eye on the hunters, too. The chimps kept quiet, as if they had seen the humans before and learned from experience what these men could be capable of. It's possible that some of their family members had been killed by hunters in the past, and now this chimp family knew what humans were and how to hide from them. Good for them! This is one family of chimps that may get to live in their forest as long as they continue to stay alert. It's kind of like the children's game of hide-and-seek, but this one is life-or-death.

How scary it would be for the young ones in these chimp families. They have to rely on the leaders, or alpha males and females, for the guidance and teamwork required to stay alive. It's like being a team, all members working as one so everyone survives and benefits.

I can just imagine the sounds of all the natural wildlife in the rainforest—loud, sharp sounds of birds, monkeys, frogs, and insects. Even leopards! Because of the humid climate, the landscape is filled with the scent of decaying leaves and plant life. The smell fills the senses. It seems like the rain forest would be a different world without the presence of humans. It would be a place where voices, vehicles, horns, telephones, and all the noises we are used to would not exist.

Well, I had better fly back. I don't want to miss anything exciting!

§ § § § §

Dr. Stephen has taken out a medication dart gun. This will be used to make Claude go to sleep; so I am just in time.

Claude has to be darted so he does not harm himself or anyone else. This is how the team will transport him to the airplane that will take him to his new home at Chimp Eden. Oh, how wonderful that sounds!

Claude has been darted now. He attempted to move forward, but he is unable to. He slumps over and sinks to the floor of his cage. It is now safe for the men to cut off the cage lock and remove him from the lonely, small jail cell in which he has been living. Jaco, Dr. Stephen, and Claude's old keeper, help to move him into the travel cage. Dr. Stephen will draw some blood so it can be sent to a lab for the blood tests, I talked about this earlier. He has to be quick, because they do not want Claude to be asleep long. The doctor has finished just in time, for Claude is waking up, safe and in his new travel cage.

Of course, he is not too happy right now, because this one is much smaller than the one he was in before. I would whisper to him to stay calm, but I do not think he will hear me over all the whooping and hollering he is doing as the men get him loaded into the vehicle.

From here, the team begins the journey to a new place called Gem Diamonds. At this compound, we will stay for several days while we wait for the blood work from Claude to come back. If he is healthy enough, he can come home with us. In the meantime, Phillip, Jaco, and the others have tried one last time to convince the owner of the two baby chimpanzees that their handling and confinement is a terrible and unnatural life. It is also dangerous for people.

Although they all have tried everything they know to convince the owner otherwise, she can only see that losing the babies would mean losing money. She would simply go back into the forest and steal more chimpanzees.

The frustrated and exhausted team has gone back to see the two little ones one last time, giving both of them treats and love before saying goodbye. These are two

chimps they will have to leave behind. I can see the disappointment and sadness on everyone's faces.

It is a quiet trip back to the compound.

§ § § § §

Good news! Claude's blood has been checked by the laboratories, and he has none of the diseases they were looking for. He is cleared for the flight to Chimp Eden.

Once again, the team and chimp are moving. This time, the South African Army is arriving in Jeeps, bringing another team member, named David. He is a photographer. I hear them calling him an *eco-warrior*. I am not sure what that means, but I think it has something to do with helping wildlife and places like the rain forest. We're heading to the army base where Claude will be loaded into the C130 airplane. He should be ready for takeoff early in the morning.

§ § § § §

It is the morning of the departure home, and I have made a big decision. I am going to sneak inside the airplane and catch a ride with the team. I am tired, and I need to get back to Jessica.

I enter the Hercules C130 and stow away in the corner near some baggage. As the engine of the enormous airplane revs up and the wheels begin to move forward, I hear shouts from the passengers aboard.

"Get going!" they yell.

The major flying this large plane puts it in full throttle, and we roll faster and faster until the wheels lift off the ground. In the distance, I can see what all the yelling is about. Several vehicles are approaching our plane to stop our flight from taking off. They have armed military guards with them, weapons drawn and ready to fire.

Wow! That was a close call. It seems we got out just in time. Don't know what that was all about, but I sure am glad we didn't stay to find out!

Now, it's time to rest and go home. The low and constant noise of the plane is calming, and I am the last to close my eyes. Claude is asleep. So are all the tired men and women on the team. This has been an adventure for sure. I do believe it is the last one I care to take.

Home sweet home. That is all I care about now.

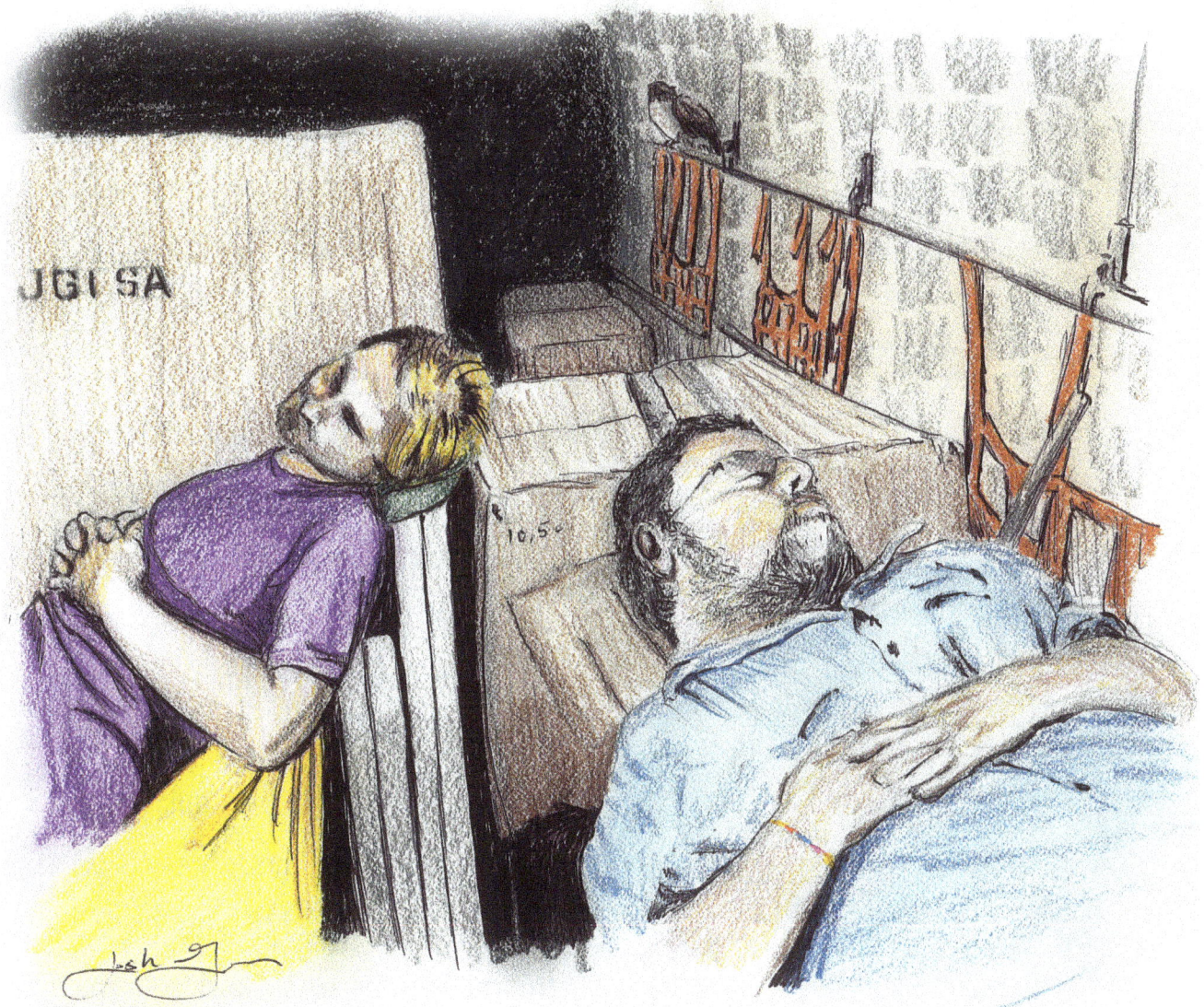

Chapter 6

Home Sweet Home

Our arrival home is a joyous occasion for everyone. After a smooth landing, compliments of the major in the South African Air Force, the huge doors of the C130 open. Flashes of light can be seen from all the people aiming their cameras on Claude and the team. Claude lets out a couple of yelps due to nervousness and the excitement of the moment. His eyes are large and dart from person to person, trying to comprehend what is happening to him. I do believe Joao or Jessica could have helped him if they had been here and could give him some reassurance.

Phillip and Jaco talk calmly to Claude, and he settles down a bit. That is, until he is loaded into the back of the truck, and then the fear

starts to show in his eyes again. But it won't take long until Claude is in his new home! He will have to go straight into isolation for three months, but from there he can hear the other chimps, and I can't imagine what a surprise that will be!

Now that the people are moving out, I can fly out of the plane without being seen, I am ready to go home. There is one more very important task to complete before I can get back to my life as it was before this mission. I must see Jessica and return the voice that was passed along for all who will listen. The gift of a VOICE is important, because more people need to understand the plight of the chimpanzee and the danger and suffering encountered by all endangered wildlife. Flying high over the sanctuary, I spot Jessica, and I will now complete my mission. *Cawwww, cawwww.*

§ § § § §

I heard the call of Moomba overhead and now the anticipation is over. The story has been told, and I've been given back the voice. I believe humans call it "sweet sorrow" when something good happens, but not everything turns out like everyone wishes. Tubo and Babush had to be left behind this time. There will be more rescues planned in the future, but everything takes time and lots of work and planning.

I have kept busy taking care of my family, and Charles has become a great dad and leader to all the younger chimps in our family. Marco really looks up to him and, even though he sometimes gets into trouble, they play often. Charles has even been tickling him, and everyone watches as they laugh and seem to really enjoy life.

Tamu is still trying hard to be the man in charge, even though he is still a baby. He gets disciplined often but, because he is stubborn, he never gives up. Tamu likes to throw tantrums by screaming and stamping his feet on the ground when he gets mad, but Charles just waits for the right time to give him a little attitude adjustment, and that takes care of things for a short time. Charles is a good leader, and Tamu is learning the ways of the chimp family. That's the way it's supposed to be.

§ § § § §

Three months have gone by now, and it's time for Claude to be introduced to his new family. It has been decided by the sanctuary manager, Phillip, that Claude will become a member of Joao's and Zac's family. I believe it will be a great fit, too!

It's funny that Claudine, the other new member of our sanctuary, was the first to go up to Claude and touch him. She was very cautious, and he did give a few slaps. But soon he realized that she was a friend, so he relaxed and began to play and enjoy her company.

It is tour time and now that Joao has gotten his snack, he comes over to our corner so we can chat a little. "Hello Jessica," he says to me.

I answer the greeting and ask him how Claude is doing.

"Very well, Jessica," he answers. "Claude is a fast learner. He seems to enjoy all the company and has started climbing trees as well as any of us. He loves the outdoors, and you should see him run! He is quite fast and gives Zac a little extra exercise. It all seems to be working out well. He seems happy and says he was so lonely in his cage at the

deserted zoo. He still has some bad dreams about those times, but it does seem that he is having them less often. Dreams…yes, I know what those dreams are like. It's not always a good thing. I hope his dreams will be happy dreams soon," Joao finishes.

As we talk and watch the rest of Joao's family, which includes Claude now, an energetic little girl and her dad come and stand very close to the fence line. I believe I hear him call her *Olivia Jane.* The girl is pointing at Claude, and he is looking their way as if maybe they had met once before. The little girl is smiling big and seems so happy. Maybe her dad is telling her Claude's story.

And so continues our lives at the sanctuary in South Africa—The Jane Goodall Institute of South Africa and Chimp Eden. Here is where a few lucky chimpanzees, like Joao and I, have found refuge. The question still remains in my mind though— is there a forest that we will be released to some day? I have heard our humans talk about this as a goal of theirs. Who is to tell what the future may bring?

For now, we are happy here at the place *WE CALL HOME.*

CLAUDE

*ALL PHOTOS COURTESY OF DAVID DEVO OOSTHUIZEN
THE JANE GOODALL INSTITUTE OF SOUTH AFRICA

COZY

JESSICA AND BABY

CHARLES

CLAUDINE

TONY GROOMING SAMPA

ZAC AND FAMILY

CLAUDE'S RESCUE

CLAUDE ON THE PLANE

JANE GOODALL

JANE AND DR. STEPHEN

THE RESCUE TEAM

ABOUT THE AUTHOR

Doreen Ingram is a retired registered nurse, foster parent for a wildlife sanctuary in her hometown, and mother of three wonderful children. Her deep love for animals led her to write her first book to support some very special chimpanzees living in a sanctuary in South Africa. From then on, she made it her goal to spread the word about the distressing plight of all great apes and other endangered wildlife.

She visits wildlife sanctuaries, volunteering whenever possible, to gain firsthand knowledge of a wide variety of animals. With this knowledge and experience, she speaks at schools, libraries, and other venues, teaching both children and adults about endangered wildlife and the sanctuaries that help them, sharing and spreading her empathy for the animals. Additionally, Doreen shares the net profits from the sale of her books and games, and from venue presentations, with the sanctuaries and organizations that help rescue and house animals in need.